Kids Knit

Baby & Kids Knitting

Copyright © 2023

All rights reserved.

DEDICATION

Contents

I. Trex Toy To Knit

MATERIALS

Patons® Canadiana™ (3.5 oz/100 g; 205 yds/187 m)

Main Color

MC Purple Glow (10753) 2 balls

Contrast A Grape Jelly (10307) 1 ball

Contrast B Winter White (10006) 1 ball

Contrast C Black (10040) 1 ball

Size U.S. 6 (4 mm) knitting needles or size needed to obtain gauge.

Stuffing.

Yarn needle.

ABBREVIATIONS

Alt = Alternate(ing)

Approx = Approximately

Beg = Beginning

Cont = Continue(ity)

Dec = Decreasing

Inc = Increasing

K = Knit

K2(3)tog = Knit next 2 (3) stitches together

Kfb = Increase 1 stitch by knitting into front and back of next stitch

M1 = Make 1 stitch by picking up horizontal loop lying before next stitch and knitting into back of loop

P = Purl

P2(3)tog = Purl next 2(3) stitches together

P2togtbl = Purl next 2 stitches together through back loops

PM = Place marker

Rem =Remaining

RS = Right side

Ssk = Slip next 2 stitches knitwise one at a time. Pass them back onto left-hand needle, then knit through back loops together

St(s) = Stitch(es)

WS = Wrong side

MEASUREMENT

Approx 20" [51 cm] high.

GAUGE

21 sts and 27 rows = 4" [10 cm] in stocking st.

INSTRUCTIONS

Note: When working with more than 1 color within a row, wind small balls of the colors to be used, one for each separate area of color in the design. Start new colors at appropriate points. To change colors, twist the two colors around each other where they meet, on WS, to avoid a hole.

Left Leg

**Sole of Foot:

With A, cast on 5 sts.

1st row: (RS). Knit. Cont in garter st (knit every row), inc 1 st at each end of next 3 rows, then on following alt rows twice. 15 sts. Cont in garter st until work from beg measures approx 3¼" [8.5 cm]. Break A. Join B.

Proceed as follows:

1st row: (RS). With B, knit.

2nd row: Purl.

Cont in stocking st, dec 1 st at each end of next row and following alt rows twice. 9 sts. Dec 1 st at each end of next 2 rows. 5 sts.

Cast off.

Top of Foot:

With MC, cast on 23 sts.

With B, cast on 28 sts.

With MC, cast on 23 sts. 74 sts.

1st row: (RS). With MC, K23. With B, K28. With MC, K23.

2nd row: With MC, P23. With B, P28. With MC, P23.

Shape toes:

3rd row: (RS). With MC, K23. *With B, K8. With MC, K2. Rep from * twice more. With MC, K21.

4th row: With MC, P23. *With B, P2tog. P4. P2togtbl. With MC, P2. Rep from * twice more. With MC, P21. 68 sts.

5th row: With MC, K23. *With B, K6. With MC, K2. Rep from * twice more. With MC, K21.

6th row: With MC, P23. *With B, P2tog. P2. P2togtbl. With MC, P2. Rep from * twice more. With MC, P21. 62 sts.

7th row: With MC, K21. (M1. K1) twice. * With B, ssk. K2tog. With MC, K1. M1. K1. Rep from * twice more.

With MC, M1. K21. 62 sts. Break B.

With MC only, starting with a purl row, work 7 rows stocking st.

Shape ankle:

Next row: (RS). K17. K2tog. (K3tog) 9 times. K16. 43 sts. Work 3 rows even.

Next row: (RS). K7. *M1. K2. Rep from * to last 8 sts. M1. K8. 58 sts.** Cont even in stocking st for another 24 rows, ending on a knit row.

Shape thigh and tail opening:

1st row: (WS). Cast off 29 sts. PM on st left on needle after cast off. Purl to end of row of row. 29 sts.

2nd row: Cast off 3 sts. K2 (including st on needle after cast off). M1. K4. M1. K3. M1. Knit to end of row of row. 29 sts.

3rd and alt rows: Purl.

4th row: Cast off 2 sts. K4 (including st left on needle after cast off). M1. K6. M1. Knit to end of row of row. 29 sts.

6th row: Cast off 2 sts. K3 (including st on needle after cast off). M1. K3. M1. K4. M1. Knit to end of row. 30 sts. Work 11 rows even, ending on a purl row. Cast on 2 sts at beg of next and following alt row. 34 sts.

Next row: (WS). Cast off 2 sts. Purl to end of row. 32 sts.

Next row: Cast on 3 sts. Knit to end of row. 35 sts. Cast off 6 sts at beg of next and every alt row until 5 sts rem. Cast off. Right Leg Work from ** to ** as given for Left Leg. Work 23 rows in stocking st, ending with purl row.

Shape thigh and tail opening:

1st row: (RS). Cast off 29 sts. PM on st left on needle after cast off. Knit to end of row. 29 sts.

2nd row: Cast off 3 sts. P2 (including st on needle after cast off). M1. P4. M1. P3. M1. Purl to end of row. 29 sts.

3rd and alt rows: Knit.

4th row: Cast off 2 sts. P4 (including st on needle after cast off). M1. P6. M1. Purl to end of row. 29 sts.

6th row: Cast off 2 sts. P3 (including st on needle after cast off). M1. P3. M1. P4. M1. Purl to end of row. 30 sts. Work 11 rows even, ending on a knit row. Cast on 2 sts at beg of next and following alt row. 34 sts.

Next row: (RS). Cast off 2 sts. Knit to end of row. 32 sts.

Next row: Cast on 3 sts. Purl to end of row. 35 sts. Cast off 6 sts beg of next and every alt row until 5 sts rem.

Purl 1 row. Cast off.

Tail

With MC, cast on 3 sts.

With A, cast on 4 sts.

With MC cast on 3 sts. 10 sts.

1st row: (RS). With MC, K3. With A K4. With MC K3.

2nd row: With MC P3. With A P4. With MC P3. Rep last 2 rows twice more.

7th row: With MC, K2. M1. K1. With A, K1. M1. K2. M1. K1. With MC, K1. M1. K2. 14 sts. Keeping colors in place, work 5 rows in stocking st.

Proceed in stocking st as follows:

13th row: (RS). With MC, K3. M1. K1. With A, K1. M1. K4. M1. K1. With MC, K1. M1. K3. 18 sts. Work 3 rows even.

17th row: With MC, K5. With A (K2tog) 4 times. With MC K5. 14 sts. Work 1 row even.

19th row: With MC, K4. M1. K1. With A, Kfb. M1. (Kfb) twice. M1. Kfb. With MC, K1. M1. K4. 22 sts. Work 3 rows even.

23rd row: With MC, K5. M1. K1. With A, K1. M1. K8. M1. K1. With MC, K1. M1. K5. 26 sts. Work 1 row even.

25th row: With MC, K7. With A, (K2tog) 6 times. With MC, K7. 20 sts. Work 1 row even.

27th row: With MC, K6. M1. K1. With A, Kfb. M1. (Kfb) 4 times. M1. Kfb. With MC, K1. M1. K6. 30 sts. Work 3 rows even.

31st row: With MC, K7. M1. K1. With A, K1. M1. K12. M1. K1. With MC, K1. M1. K7. 34 sts. Work 1 row even.

33rd row: With MC, K9. With A, (K2tog) 8 times. With MC, K9. 26 sts. Work 1 row even.

35th row: With MC, K8. M1. K1. With A, Kfb. M1. (Kfb) 6 times. M1. Kfb. With MC, K1. M1. K8. 38 sts. Work 3 rows even.

39th row: With MC, K9. M1. K1. With A, K1. M1. K16. M1. K1. With MC, K1. M1. K9. 42 sts. Work 1 row even.

41st row: With MC, K11. With A, (K2tog) 10 times. With MC, K11. 32 sts. Work 1 row even.

43rd row: With MC, K10. M1. K1. With A, Kfb. M1. (Kfb) 8 times. M1. Kfb. With MC, K1. M1. K10. 46 sts. Work 3 rows even.

47th row: With MC, K11. M1. K1. With A, K1. M1. K20. M1. K1. With MC, K1. M1. K11. 50 sts. Work 1 row even.

49th row: With MC, K13. With A, (K2tog) 12 times. With MC, K13. 38 sts. Work 1 row even.

51st row: With MC, K12. M1. K1. With A, Kfb. M1. (Kfb) 10 times. M1. Kfb. With MC, K1. M1. K12. 54 sts. Work 1 row even.

53rd row: With MC, K13. M1. K1. With A, K1. M1. K24. M1. K1. With A, K1. M1. K13. 58 sts. Work 1 row even.

55th row: With MC, K14. M1. K1. With A, K1. M1. K26. M1. K1. With MC, K1. M1. K14. 62 sts. Work 1 row even.

57th row: With MC, K8. PM for Chart I between last 2 sts. K7. *M1. K1. With A, (K2tog) 15 times. With MC, K1. M1. Rep from * to * once more. 49 sts. Work 1 row even.

59th row: With MC, K16. M1. K1. With A, (Kfb. M1) twice. (Kfb) 11 times. (M1. Kfb) twice. With MC, K1. M1. K16. 70 sts. Work 3 rows even. Keeping colors correct, cast off 6 sts beg next 10 rows. Cast off rem 10 sts.

Gusset

With A, cast on 26 sts. Beg with a knit row, work 2 rows stocking st. Cont in stocking st, dec 1 st each end of next 9 rows, then on following alt row. 6 sts. Work 3 rows even.

Next row: (RS). Kfb. Knit to last 2 sts. Kfb. K1.

Next row: Purl.

Inc 1 st at each end of next 5 rows, then on following alt rows 4 times. 26 sts.

Work 1 row even.

PM at each end of last row. Inc 1 st at each end of next and following alt rows twice, then on following 4th row.

Work 3 rows even.

Leave rem 34 sts on a spare needle.

Sew Gusset to front of Thighs, matching top edges and matching markers on Gusset to markers on Legs.

Sew rem of Gusset to cast off sts of Legs.

Upper Body

With RS facing and MC, pick up and knit 37 sts across top of shaped edge of left Thigh.

with A, 34 sts across top of Gusset, with MC, 37 sts up shaped edge of right Thigh to top. 108 sts.

Next row: With MC, P30. With A, P47. With MC, P30. Keeping colors in place, work 2 rows stocking st.

Proceed as follows:

1st row: (RS). With MC, K30. With A, K48. With MC, K30.

2nd and alt rows: Purl, keeping colors in place.

3rd row: With MC, K28. K2tog. With A, ssk. K44. K2tog. With MC, ssk. K28. 104 sts.

5th row: With MC, K29. With A, K1. (K2tog. K1) 15 times. With MC, K29. 89 sts.

7th row: With MC, K27. K2tog. With A, K3. (Kfb. K1) 13 times. K2. With MC, ssk. K27. 100 sts.

9th row: With MC, K28. With A, K44. With MC, K28.

11th row: With MC, K26. K2tog. With A, ssk. K40. K2tog. With MC, ssk. K26. 96 sts.

13th row: With MC, K27. With A, ssk. (K2tog. K1) 12 times. (K2tog) twice. With MC, K27. 81 sts.

15th row: With MC, K25. K2tog. With A, K1. (Kfb. K1) 13 times. With MC, ssk. K25. 92 sts.

17th row: With MC, K26. With A, K40. With MC, K26.

19th row: With MC, K24. K2tog. With A, ssk. K36. K2tog. With MC, ssk. K24. 88 sts.

21st row: With MC, K25. With A, K1. (K2tog. K1. K2tog) 7 times. K2. With MC, K25. 74 sts.

23rd row: With MC, K23. K2tog. With A, K3. *(Kfb) twice. K1. Rep from * 5 times more. K3. With MC, ssk. K23. 84 sts.

25th row: With MC, K24. With A, K36. With MC, K24.

27th row: With MC, K22. K2tog. With A, ssk. K32. K2tog. With MC, ssk. K22. 80 sts.

29th row: With MC, K10. K2tog. K9. K2tog. With A, (K2tog) 17 times. With MC. ssk. K9. ssk. K10. 59 sts.

31st row: With MC, K8. K2tog. K9. K2tog. With A, K2. (Kfb) 13 times. K2. With MC, ssk. K9. ssk. K8. 68 sts.

33rd row: With MC, K8. K2tog. K7. K2tog. With A, K30. With MC, ssk. K7. ssk. K8. 64 sts.

35th row: With MC, K8. K2tog. K5. K2tog. With A, K30. With MC, ssk. K5. ssk. K8. 60 sts.

37th row: With MC, K15. With A, (K2tog) 15 times. With MC, K15. 45 sts.

39th row: With MC, K15. With A, K2. (Kfb) 11 times. K2. With MC, K15. 56 sts.

41st and 43rd rows: With MC, K15. With A, K26. With MC, K15. 45th row: With MC, K15. With A, (K2tog) 13 times. With MC, K15. 43 sts.

47th row: With MC, K15. With A, (Kfb) 13 times. With MC, K15. 56 sts. Work 5 rows even.

Shape neck:

Next row: (RS). Keeping colors in place, K28. Turn. Leave rem sts on a spare needle Cont on these 28 sts as follows: Cast off 4 sts beg next row, then cast off 3 sts beg every following alt row until 15 sts rem.

Next row: (RS). K9. PM between last 2 sts for Chart I. K6. PM on last st for Head. Work 5 rows even. Dec 1 st at end of next and every alt row until 9 sts rem, then at same edge on next 3 rows. 6 sts. Cast off. With RS facing, rejoin A to rem sts. Cast off 4 sts. Keeping colors correct, knit to end of row. 24 sts. Work 1 row even. Cast off 3 sts beg of next and every following alt row until 15 sts rem. Work 1 row even.

Next row: K1. PM on last st for Head. K7. PM between last 2 sts for spots. K7. Work 5 rows even. Dec 1 st at beg of next and every alt row until 9 sts rem, then at same edge on next 3 rows. 6 sts.

Cast off.

Fold

Neck in half to form a tube. Sew back neck seam tog for 1¼" [3 cm] from top where sts were cast off.

Head

With RS of work facing and MC, pick up and knit 20 sts up right side of head from second marker and across cast off sts to back neck seam, then 20 sts across cast off sts and down left side of head to first marker. 40 sts.

Next row: (WS). Purl. Beg with a knit row, work in stocking st and cast on 3 sts beg of next 6 rows, then cast on 4 sts at beg of following 2 rows. 66 sts. Work 1 row even.

Next row: (WS). P21. PM on last st for Chart IV. P25. PM on last st for Chart V. P20.

Shape eyes:

Next row: (RS). K27. *(Kfb) 4 times. K4. Rep from * once more. K23. 82 sts.

Next row: P26. PM on last st for Chart II. P31. PM on last st for Chart III. P25. Work 5 rows even.

Next row: P27. *(P3tog) 4 times. P4. Rep from * once more. P23. 66 sts. Work 8 rows even.

Next row: K2tog. K2. *K2tog. K3. Rep from * to last 2 sts. K2tog. 52 sts. Work 9 rows even.

Next row: K12. K2tog. (K3tog) 8 times. K2tog. K12. 34 sts. Next row: Purl.

Next row: (K3tog) 4 times. K2tog. K6. K2tog. (K3tog) 4 times. 16 sts. Next row: Purl.

Cast off.

Arms (make 2 alike)

With B, cast on 7 sts and purl 1 row.

Next row: (RS). (Kfb) 7 times. 14 sts. Beg with a purl row, work 3 rows in stocking st.

Break B. With MC work 5 rows in stocking st.

Next row: (WS). P8. PM between last 2 sts. P6. Work 4 rows even. Inc 1 st at each end of next and every following 4th row until there are 22 sts. Work 3 rows even.

Shape top:

Cast off 4 sts beg of next 4 rows.

Cast off rem 6 sts.

FINISHING

With C, work Chart I, duplicate st spots on each side of Neck and Tail, below markers.

With 2 strands of B and C, using markers for eyes on head as a guide, duplicate st eyes from Charts II and III. With strands of B, using markers for teeth on head as a guide, duplicate st teeth from charts IV and V.

With C used double, duplicate st on either side of nose for nostrils as illustrated. Secure a boll of stuffing into each eye with small stitches, to make them protrude. Join under seam of head, then sew cast on sts of head to cast off sts of neck. Place center of cast off edge of nose to head seam and join seam at end of nose.

With C, embroider mouth in stem st as illustrated. Join back seam of each leg. Sew soles of feet to base of legs, matching top part of soles to toes of legs. Join tail seam. Sew tail in place all round tail opening. Join neck and back seam, leaving an opening at base for stuffing. Stuff toy and sew opening closed. Raised spots (make 12)

With C, cast on 7 sts. Work in garter st (knit every row), dec 1 st each end of 3rd and 4th rows. Cast off rem 3 sts. Sew cast on edge of spots to back of Toy, first to come ¾" [2 cm] from end of tail and rem spaced evenly between. Sew arm seams. Sew cast on edges of arms, matching seam to center of cast on edge. Stuff arms lightly. Sew a tight running st through both thicknesses of arm from center of cast on edge to marker, forming 2 fingers. Sew arms to each side of body as illustrated.'

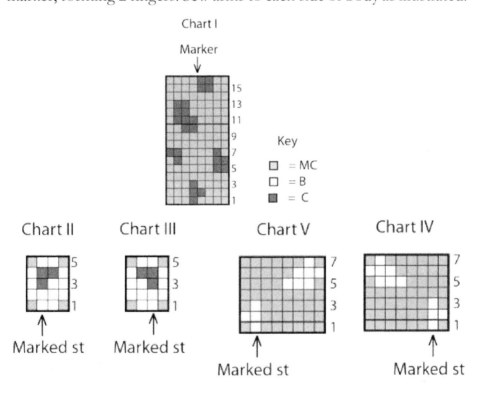

Chart I

Marker

Key

☐ = MC
☐ = B
■ = C

Chart II

Chart III

Chart V

Chart IV

Marked st

Marked st

Marked st

Marked st

II. Child's Knit Crew Neck Pullover

MATERIALS

Sizes 2 4 6 8 10 Caron® Simply Soft® (Solids: 6 oz/170.1 g; 315 yds/288 m; Heathers: 5 oz/141 g; 250 yds/228 m)

Chartreuse (39771) 2 2 3 3 4 balls

OR Caron® Simply Soft® Tweeds™ (5 oz/141.1 g; 250 yds/228 m)

Off White (23001) 2 2 3 3 4 balls

Sizes U.S. 7 (4.5 mm) and U.S. 8 (5 mm) knitting needles or size

needed to obtain gauge.

4 stitch holders.

ABBREVIATIONS

Beg = Begin(ning)

Cont = Continue(ity)

Dec = Decrease(ing)

Inc = Increase(ing)

K = Knit

K2tog = Knit next 2 stitches together

P = Purl

P2tog = Purl next 2 stitches together

P2togtbl = Purl next 2 stitches together through back loops

Rem = Remain(ing)

Rep = Repeat

RS = Right side

Ssk = Slip next 2 stitches knitwise one at a time. Pass them back onto

left-hand needle, then knit through back loops together

St(s) = Stitch(es)

SIZES

To fit bust measurement

2 21" [53.5 cm]

4 23" [58.5 cm]

6 25" [63.5 cm]

8 26½" [67.5 cm]

10 28" [71 cm]

Finished bust

2 26" [66 cm]

4 28" [71 cm]

6 30" [76 cm]

8 32" [81.5 cm]

10 34" [86.5 cm]

GAUGE

18 sts and 24 rows = 4" [10 cm] in stocking st with larger needles.

INSTRUCTIONS

The instructions are written for smallest size.

If changes are necessary for larger sizes the instructions will be written thus ( ).

Numbers for each size are shown in the same color throughout the pattern.

When only one number is given in black, it applies to all sizes.

BACK

**With smaller needles cast on 58 (62-66-70-74) sts.

1st row: (RS). *K2. P2. Rep from * to last 2 sts. K2.

2nd row: *P2. K2. Rep from * to last 2 sts. P2. Rep last 2 rows (K2. P2) ribbing for 2 (2-2-2½-2½)" [5 (5-5-6-6) cm], ending on a 2nd row and inc 1 (1- 3-3-3) st(s) evenly across last row. 59 (63-69-73-77) sts.

Change to larger needles and proceed in stocking st until work from beg measures 9 (10- 11-11½-12½)" [23 (25.5-28- 29-32) cm], ending on a purl row.

Shape raglans:

Cast off 2 (2-2- 3-3) sts beg next 2 rows. 55 (59- 65-67-71) sts.

Sizes 2, 4, 6 and 8 only:

Next row: (RS). K2. ssk. Knit to last 4 sts. K2tog. K2.

Next row: P2. P2tog. Purl to last 4 sts. P2togtbl. P2.

All sizes:

1st row: (RS). K2. ssk. Knit to last 4 sts. K2tog. K2.

2nd row: Purl.** Rep last 2 rows 14 (15-17-18-21) times more.

Leave rem 21 (23-25- 25-27) sts on a st holder.

FRONT

Work from ** to ** as given for Back. Rep last 2 rows 7 (8-9-10-13) times more. 35 (37-41-43-43) sts.

Shape neck:

1st row: (RS). K2. ssk. K8 (8-10-10-12) (neck edge). Turn.

2nd row: Purl.

3rd row: K2. ssk. Knit to last 2 sts. K2tog. Rep last 2 rows 2 (2-3-3-4) times more. 5 sts rem.

Next row: P5.

Next row: K1. ssk. K2tog.

Next row: P3.

Next row: K1. ssk.

Next row: P2.

Next row: ssk.

Fasten off.

With RS facing, slip next 11 (13-13- 15-11) sts onto a st holder.

1st row: (RS). Rejoin yarn to rem sts. Knit to last 4 sts. K2tog. K2.

2nd row: Purl.

3rd row: ssk. Knit to last 4 sts. K2tog. K2. Rep last 2 rows 2 (2-3-3-4) times more. 5 sts rem.

Next row: P5.

Next row: ssk. K2tog. K1.

Next row: P3.

Next row: K2tog. K1.

Next row: P2.

Next row: K2tog.

Fasten off.

SLEEVES

With smaller needles, cast on 34 (34-38-38-42) sts.

Work 2 (2-2-2½-2½)" [5 (5-5- 6-6) cm] in (K2. P2) ribbing as given for Back, ending on a 2nd row and inc 3 (3-3-3-1) st(s) evenly across last row. 37 (37-41-41-43) sts.

Change to larger needles and work 6 rows in stocking st. Inc 1 st each end of next row and following 6th (4th-4th4th-4th) rows until there are 45 (43-47-55-55) sts.

Sizes 4, 6, 8 and 10 only: Inc 1 st each end of following 6th rows until there are (49-55-59-63) sts.

All sizes: Cont even until work from beg measures 7½ (9½- 10½- 11½-12½)" [19 (24-26.5- 29-32) cm], ending on a purl row.

Shape raglans: Cast off 2 (2-2- 3-3) sts beg next 2 rows. 41 (45- 51-53-57) sts.

1st row: (RS). K2. ssk. Knit to last 4 sts. K2tog. K2.

2nd row: P2. P2tog. Purl to last 4 sts. P2togtbl. P2.

3rd row: As 1st row.

4th row: Purl. Rep last 4 rows 0 (1-2-1-1) time(s) more. 35 (33-33-41-45) sts.

1st row: (RS). K2. ssk. Knit to last 4 sts. K2tog. K2.

2nd row: Purl. Rep last 2 rows 13 (12-12-15-17) times more.

Leave rem 7 (7-7- 9-9) sts on a st holder.

FINISHING

Sew raglan seams leaving left back raglan seam open.

Neckband:

With RS facing and smaller needles, K7 (7-7-9-9) from Left Sleeve st holder, dec 1 st at center.

Pick up and knit 11 (11-12- 12-14) sts down Left Front neck edge.

K11 (13-13-15-11) from Front st holder.

Pick up and knit 11 (11-12-12-14) sts up Right Front neck edge. K7 (7-7-9-9) from Right Sleeve st holder, dec 1 st at center.

K21 (23-25-25-27) from Back st holder, dec 0 (0-0-2-0) sts evenly across. 66 (70-74-78-82) sts.

Beg on a 2nd row, work 7 rows in (K2. P2) ribbing as given for Back.

Cast off loosely in ribbing.

Sew left back raglan and neckband seam. Sew side and sleeve seams.

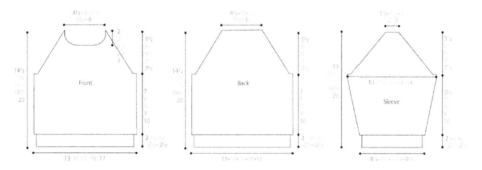

III. Rosy Set

1. Blanket

SIZES

Actual Completed Blanket is 55 cm, 21½ in, wide measurement and 80 cm, 31½ in, long

YOU WILL NEED

1 50g balls of Paintbox Yarns Baby DK (As seen on cover) .

4 × Ballet Pink 1 Pair of 3¾mm (UK 9 – US 5) knitting needles

1 Pair of 4mm (UK 8 – US 6) knitting needles

TENSION (GAUGE)

22 stitches and 30 rows to 10 cm, 4 in, measured over stocking (stockinette) stitch using 4mm (UK 8 – US 6) needles, or size required to give correct tension. It is vitally important to check your tension (gauge) before starting as working to the wrong tension (gauge) will mean your item will not be the size shown and could result in yarn being left over, or more yarn being required. Before beginning, knit a tension (gauge) swatch at least 13 cm, 5 in, square and measure your tension (gauge). If there are more sts and rows than stated, try again using thicker needles. If there are fewer sts and rows than stated, try again using thinner needles.

GOOD TO KNOW

1 Paintbox Yarns cannot accept responsibility for the finished item if any yarn other than the recommended yarn is used.

l Yarn quantities are based on average requirements and are therefore approximate.

l Colour reproduction is as close as printing processes will allow.

l Instructions are written using UK terminology with changes for US terminology given in italics in round brackets ( ) afterwards.

l Repeat figures in round brackets ( ) the number of times stated afterwards.

ABBREVIATIONS

Cm = centimetres

Cont = continue

In = inches

K = knit

P = purl

Patt = pattern

Psso = pass slipped stitch over

Rep = repeat

Rs = right side

Sl 1 = slip one stitch

St st (stockinette st) = stocking stitch (stockinette stitch) (k on rs rows, p on ws rows)

St(s) = stitch(es)

Tog = together

Ws = wrong side

Yfwd = yarn forward.

Rosebud 5 sts = over next 5 sts, 3 long loops are pulled up to form rosebud effect.

Work these 5 sts as follows: K1, insert right needle point into centre of 3rd st of this group of 5 sts but 4 rows below and draw a loop through and leave this loop on right needle, K2, insert right needle point into centre of same st as used for last long loop and draw a 2nd loop through and leave this loop on right needle, K2, insert right needle point into centre of same st as used for last long loop and draw a 3rd loop through and leave this loop on right needle.

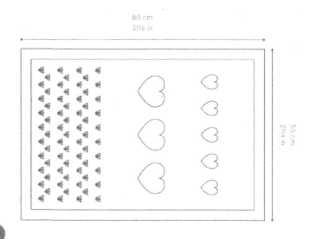

Instructions

Cast on 121 sts using 3¾mm (UK 9 – US 5) needles.

Row 1 (rs) k1, *p1, k1, rep from * to end.

Row 2 as row 1.

These 2 rows form moss st. Work in moss st for a further 12 rows, ending with a ws row.

Change to 4mm (UK 8 – US 6) needles.

Now work in patt as follows:

Row 15 (rs) moss st 9 sts, K to last 9 sts, moss st 9 sts.

Row 16 moss st 9 sts, P to last 9 sts, moss st 9 sts.

Rows 17 to 22 as rows 15 and 16, 3 times.

Now work rosebud border patt as follows: rows 23 to 26 as rows 15 and 16, twice.

Row 27 moss st 9 sts, K4, (rosebud 5 sts, K5) 9 times, rosebud 5 sts, K4, moss st 9 sts. Row 28 moss st 9 sts, P4, *(P tog drawn up loop of previous row and next st, P1) twice, P tog drawn up loop of previous row and next st, P5, rep from * to last 18 sts, (P tog drawn up loop of previous row and next st, P1) twice, P tog drawn up loop of previous row and next st, P4, moss st 9 sts.

Rows 29 to 32 as rows 15 and 16, twice.

Row 33 moss st 9 sts, K9, (rosebud 5 sts, K5) 9 times, K4, moss st 9 sts.

Row 34 moss st 9 sts, P9, *(P tog drawn up loop of previous row and next st, P1) twice, P tog drawn up loop of previous row and next st, P5, rep from * to last 13 sts, P4, moss st 9 sts.

Now rep rows 17 to 34 twice more, then rows 17 to 28 again.

This completes rosebud border patt. Now rep rows 15 and 16 until Blanket measures 36 cm, 14 in, ending with a ws row.

Now place **Moss st Heart Motifs** as follows: next (rs) moss st 9 sts, K8, (work next 23 sts as row 1 of Moss st Heart Motif Chart, K9) twice, work next 23 sts as row 1 of Moss st Heart Motif Chart, K8, moss st 9 sts. Next row moss st 9 sts, P8, (work next 23 sts as row 2

of Moss st Heart Motif Chart, P9) twice, work next 23 sts as row 2 of
Moss st Heart Motif Chart, P8, moss st 9 sts.

These 2 rows set the sts – 3 Moss st

Heart Motifs with st st (stockinette st) between and at sides, and edge

9 sts still in moss st.

Cont as now set until all 27 rows of Moss st

Heart Motifs have been completed, ending with a rs row.

Next row (ws) as row 16.

Now rep rows 15 and 16 until

Blanket measures 58 cm, 22¾ in, ending with a ws row.

Now place

Lacy Heart Motifs as follows: next row (rs) moss st 9 sts, K7, (work
next 13 sts as row 1 of Lacy Heart Motif Chart, K6) 5 times, K1,
moss st 9 sts. next row moss st 9 sts, P7, (work next 13 sts as row 2
of Lacy Heart Motif Chart, P6) 5 times, P1, moss st 9 sts.

These 2 rows set the sts – 5

Lacy Heart Motifs with st st (stockinette st) between and at sides, and
edge 9 sts still in moss st. Cont as now set until all 16 rows of Lacy
Heart Motifs have been completed, ending with a ws row.

Now rep rows 15 and 16 until Blanket measures 76 cm, 30 in, ending with a ws row.

Change to 3¾mm (UK 9 – US 5) needles. Now work all sts in moss st as given for cast-on edge for 14 rows, ending with a ws row.

Cast (bind) off in moss st

MAKING UP

Do NOT steam press! Pin out Blanket to measurements given, cover with a clean damp cloth and leave to dry naturally.

Lacy Heart Motip

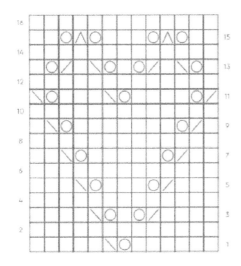

Key

K on rs rows,
P on ws rows

☒ P on rs rows,
K on ws rows

○ yfwd

╱ K2tog

╲ sl 1, K1, psso

∧ sl 1, K2tog, psso

Moss St Heart Motif

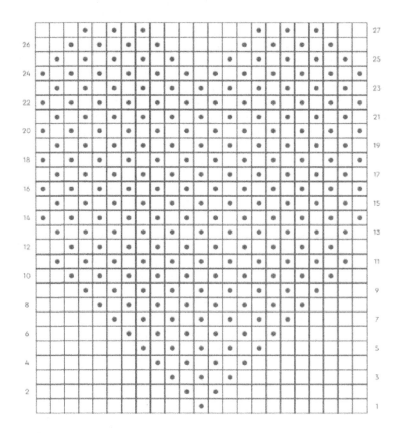

2. Bonnet

SIZES

To fit age 0-3 3-6 6 12 12-18 months Width around 33 36 39 41 cm face 13 14 15½ 16 in

YOU WILL NEED

50g balls of Paintbox Yarns Baby DK (As seen on cover) . 1 [1: 1: 1]

× Ballet Pink

Pair of 3¼mm (UK 10 – US 3) knitting needles

Pair of 4mm (UK 8 – US 6) knitting needles

50 cm, 19½ in, long of 15 mm, ½ in, wide ribbon

TENSION (GAUGE)

22 stitches and 30 rows to 10 cm, 4 in, measured over stocking (stockinette) stitch using 4mm (UK 8 – US 6) needles, or size required to give correct tension. It is vitally important to check your tension (gauge) before starting as working to the wrong tension (gauge) will mean your item will not be the size shown and could result in yarn being left over, or more yarn being required. Before beginning, knit a tension (gauge) swatch at least 13 cm, 5 in, square and measure your tension (gauge). If there are more sts and rows than stated, try again using thicker needles. If there are fewer sts and rows than stated, try again using thinner needles.

GOOD TO KNOW

Paintbox Yarns cannot accept responsibility for the finished item if any yarn other than the recommended yarn is used.

Yarn quantities are based on average requirements and are therefore approximate.

Colour reproduction is as close as printing processes will allow.

Instructions are written using UK terminology with changes for US terminology given in italics in round brackets ( ) afterwards.

Repeat figures in round brackets ( ) the number of times stated afterwards.

Instructions are given for the smallest size, with changes for the larger sizes given in square brackets [ ] afterwards.

Where only one figure is given, this relates to all sizes.

Where the figure 0 appears, no stitches, times or rows are worked for this size.

ABBREVIATIONS

Beg = beginning;

Cm = centimetres;

Cont = continue;

Dec = decreas(e)(ing);

In = inches;

Inc = increas(e)(ing);

K = knit;

P = purl;

Psso = pass slipped stitch over;

Rem = remain(s)(ing);

Rep = repeat;

Rs = right side;

Sl 1 = slip one stitch;

St st (stockinette st) = stocking stitch (stockinette stitch) (k on rs rows, p on ws rows);

St(s) = stitch(es);

Tog = together;

Ws = wrong side;

Yfwd = yarn forward.

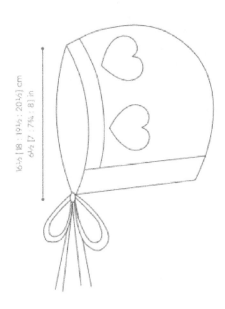

16½ [18 : 19½ : 20½] cm
6½ [7 : 7¾ : 8] in

Instructions

Cast on 72 [80: 84: 92] sts using 3¼mm (UK 10 – US 3) needles.

Row 1 (rs) K3, *P2, K2, rep from * to last st, K1.

Row 2 K1, P2, *K2, P2, rep from * to last st, K1. These 2 rows form rib. Work in rib for 4 rows more, inc [dec: inc: dec] 1 st at centre of last row and ending with a ws row. 73 [79: 85: 91] sts.

Change to 4mm (UK 8 – US 6) needles.

Beg with a K row, work in st st (stockinette st) for 2 rows, ending with a ws row.

Now place Heart Motifs as follows:

Row 1 (rs) K6 [9: 9: 12], *work next 13 sts as row 1 of Heart Motif Chart, K3 [3: 5: 5], rep from * twice more, work next 13 sts as row 1 of Heart Motif Chart, K6 [9: 9: 12].

Row 2 P6 [9: 9: 12], *work next 13 sts as row 2 of Heart Motif Chart, P3 [3: 5: 5], rep from * twice more, work next 13 sts as row 2 of Heart Motif Chart, P6 [9: 9: 12]. These 2 rows set the sts – 4 Heart Motifs with st st (stockinette st) between and at sides. Keeping sts correct as now set, cont until all 16 rows of Heart Motifs have been completed, ending with a ws row.

Cont straight in st st (stockinette st) until Bonnet measures 11 [12: 12: 13] cm, 4¼ [4¾: 4¾: 5] in, ending with a ws row.

Place markers at both ends of last row.

Shape back of head

Row 1 (rs) K1, (k2tog, K4) 12 [13: 14: 15] times. 61 [66: 71: 76] sts. Work 3 rows.

Row 5 (K3, sl 1, K1, psso) 12 [13: 14: 15] times, K1. 49 [53: 57: 61] sts. Work 3 rows.

Row 9 K1, (k2tog, K2) 12 [13: 14: 15] times. 37 [40: 43: 46] sts. Work 1 row.

Row 11 (K1, sl 1, K1, psso) 12 [13: 14: 15] times, K1. 25 [27: 29: 31] sts. Work 1 row.

Row 13 K1, (k2tog) 12 [13: 14: 15] times. Break yarn and thread through rem 13 [14: 15: 16] sts. Pull up tight and fasten off securely.

Neck edging

Join back seam of Bonnet from fasten-off point to markers along row-end edges. With rs facing and using 3¼mm (UK 10 – US 3) needles, starting and ending at cast-on edge, pick up and k25 [27: 27: 29] sts along row-end edge to seam, 1 st from seam, and 25 [27: 27: 29] sts along other row-end edge. 51 [55: 55: 59] sts.

Row 1 (ws) K1, *P1, K1, rep from * to end.

Row 2 K2, *P1, K1, rep from * to last st, K1. These 2 rows form rib. Work in rib for a further 3 rows, ending with a ws row. Cast (bind) off in rib.

MAKING UP

Do NOT steam press! Cut ribbon into 2 equal lengths and attach one end of each piece to row-end edge of Neck Edging. Tie ends in a bow under chin. Pin out Bonnet to measurements given, cover with a clean damp cloth and leave to dry naturally

HEART MOTIF CHART

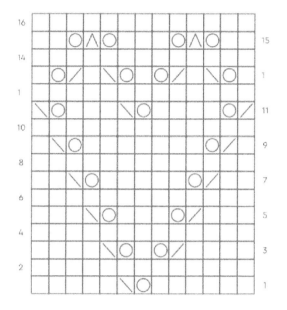

Key

☐ K on rs rows,
  P on ws rows
Ⓞ yfwd
⧄ K2tog
⧅ sl 1, K1, psso
⋀ sl 1, K2tog, psso

3. Bootees

SIZES

To fit age 0-3 3-6 6-12 12-18 months Length of 8½ 9 9½ 10 cm foot 3¼ 3½ 3¾ 4 in

YOU WILL NEED

1 50g balls of Paintbox Yarns Baby DK (As seen on cover) . 1 [1: 1: 1] × Ballet Pink 1 Pair of 3¼mm (UK 10 – US 3) knitting needles 1 Pair of 4mm (UK 8 – US 6) knitting needles

TENSION (GAUGE)

22 stitches and 30 rows to 10 cm, 4 in, measured over stocking (stockinette) stitch using 4mm (UK 8 – US 6) needles, or size required to give correct tension.

It is vitally important to check your tension (gauge) before starting as working to the wrong tension (gauge) will mean your item will not be the size shown and could result in yarn being left over, or more yarn being required.

Before beginning, knit a tension (gauge) swatch at least 13 cm, 5 in, square and measure your tension (gauge). If there are more sts and rows than stated, try again using thicker needles. If there are fewer sts and rows than stated, try again using thinner needles.

GOOD TO KNOW

l Paintbox Yarns cannot accept responsibility for the finished item if any yarn other than the recommended yarn is used.

l Yarn quantities are based on average requirements and are therefore approximate.

l Colour reproduction is as close as printing processes will allow.

l Instructions are written using UK terminology with changes for US terminology given in italics in round brackets ( ) afterwards.

l Repeat figures in round brackets ( ) the number of times stated afterwards.

l Instructions are given for the smallest size, with changes for the larger sizes given in square brackets [ ] afterwards.

l Where only one figure is given, this relates to all sizes.

l Where the figure 0 appears, no stitches, times or rows are worked for this size.

ABBREVIATIONS

Beg = beginning;

Cm = centimetres;

In = inches;

Inc = increas(e)(ing);

K = knit;

M1 = make one stitch by picking up loop lying between needles and working into back of this loop;

P = purl;

Rem = remain(s)(ing);

Psso = pass slipped stitch over;

Rs = right side;

Sl 1 = slip one stitch;

St st (stockinette st) = stocking stitch (stockinette stitch) (k on rs rows, p on ws rows);

St(s) = stitch(es);

Tog = together;

Ws = wrong side.

Rosebud 5 sts = over next 5 sts, 3 long loops are pulled up to form rosebud effect.

Work these 5 sts as follows: K1, insert right needle point into centre of 3rd st of this group of 5 sts but 4 rows below and draw a loop through and leave this loop on right needle, K2, insert right needle point into centre of same st as used for last long loop and draw a 2nd loop through and leave this loop on right needle, K2, insert right needle point into centre of same st as used for last long loop and draw a 3rd loop through and leave this loop on right needle.

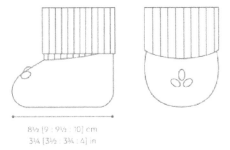

8½ [9 : 9½ : 10] cm
3¼ [3½ : 3¾ : 4] in

Instructions

Cast on 17 [21: 25: 29] sts using 4mm (UK 8 – US 6) needles.

Row 1 (ws) purl.

Row 2 (k1, m1) twice, k5 [7: 8: 10], m1, k1, m1, k1 [1: 3: 3], m1, k1, m1, k5 [7: 8: 10], (m1, k1) twice. 25 [29: 33: 37] sts.

Row 3 purl.

Row 4 k2, m1, k1, m1, k7 [9: 10: 12], m1, k1, m1, k3 [3: 5: 5], m1, k1, m1, k7 [9: 10: 12], m1, k1, m1, k2. 33 [37: 41: 45] sts.

Row 5 purl.

Row 6 k3, m1, k1, m1, k9 [11: 12: 14], m1, k1, m1, k5 [5: 7: 7], m1, k1, m1, k9 [11: 12: 14], m1, k1, m1, k3. 41 [45: 49: 53] sts. Beg with a p row, work in st st (stockinette st) for 5 [7: 7: 9] rows, ending with a ws row.

Shape top of foot

Row 1 (rs) K24 [26: 29: 31], sl 1, k2tog, psso and turn.

Row 2 sl 1, P7 [7: 9: 9], p3tog and turn.

Row 3 sl 1, K7 [7: 9: 9], sl 1, k2tog, psso and turn. Row 4 sl 1, P7 [7: 9: 9], p3tog and turn. Rep last 2 rows 0 [1: 1: 2] times more.

Next row (rs) sl 1, K1 [1: 2: 2], rosebud 5 sts, K1 [1: 2: 2], sl 1, k2tog, psso and turn.

Next row sl 1, P1 [1: 2: 2], (P tog drawn up loop of previous row and next st, P1) twice, P tog drawn up loop of previous row and next st, P1 [1: 2: 2], p3tog and turn. Next row sl 1, K7 [7: 9: 9], (sl 1, k2tog, psso) 1 [0: 1: 0] times, (sl 1, K1, psso) 0 [1: 0: 1] times and turn. Next row sl 1, P7 [7: 9: 9], (p3tog) 1 [0: 1: 0] times, (p2tog) 0 [1: 0: 1] times and turn.

Next row sl 1, K to end. 25 [27: 29: 31] sts. This completes shaping for top of foot. Beg with a P row, work in st st (stockinette st) across all sts for 3 rows, inc 1 [3: 1: 3] sts evenly across last row. 26 [30: 30: 34] sts. Change to 3¼mm (UK 10 – US 3) needles. Next row (rs) K2, *P2, K2, rep from * to end. Next row P2, *K2, P2, rep from * to end. Last 2 rows form rib. Cont in rib for a further 16 [18: 18: 20] rows, ending with a ws row. Cast (bind) of loosely in rib.

MAKING UP

Do NOT steam press! Join sole and back seam, reversing seam for last 12 rows (for turn back). Fold rib cuff in half to outside. Pin out Bootee to measurements given, cover with a clean damp cloth and leave to dry naturally.

4. Matinee Jacket

SIZES

To fit age 0-3 3-6 6-12 12-18 months

To fit chest 41 46 51 56 cm 16 18 20 22 in

Actual measurement 45 50 55 61 cm (at underarm)

17½ 19½ 21¾ 24 in

Finished length 24 28 32 36 cm 9½ 11 12½ 14 in

Sleeve seam 12 15 19 23 cm

4¾ 6 7½ 9 in

YOU WILL NEED

1 50g balls of Paintbox Yarns Baby DK (As seen on cover) . 2[2: 3: 3] × Ballet Pink

1 Pair of 3¼mm (UK 10 – US 3) knitting needles

1 Pair of 3¾mm (UK 9 – US 5) knitting needles

1 Pair of 4mm (UK 8 – US 6) knitting needles

1 1 × button approx 15mm, ½in

TENSION (GAUGE)

22 stitches and 30 rows to 10 cm, 4 in, measured over stocking (stockinette) stitch using 4mm (UK 8 – US 6) needles, or size required to give correct tension. It is vitally important to check your tension (gauge) before starting as working to the wrong tension (gauge) will mean your item will not be the size shown and could result in yarn being left over, or more yarn being required. Before

beginning, knit a tension (gauge) swatch at least 13 cm, 5 in, square and measure your tension (gauge).

If there are more sts and rows than stated, try again using thicker needles.

If there are fewer sts and rows than stated, try again using thinner needles.

GOOD TO KNOW

l Paintbox Yarns cannot accept responsibility for the finished garment if any yarn other than the recommended yarn is used.

l Yarn quantities are based on average requirements and are therefore approximate.

l Colour reproduction is as close as printing processes will allow.

l Instructions are written using UK terminology with changes for US terminology given in italics in round brackets ( ) afterwards.

l Repeat figures in round brackets ( ) the number of times stated afterwards.

l Instructions are given for the smallest size, with changes for the larger sizes given in square brackets [ ] afterwards.

l Where only one figure is given, this relates to all sizes.

l Where the figure 0 appears, no stitches, times or rows are worked for this size.

ABBREVIATIONS

Alt = alternate;

Beg = beginning;

Cm = centimetres;

Cont = continue;

Dec = decreas(e)(ing);

Foll = following;

G st = garter stitch;

In = inches;

Inc = increas(e)(ing);

K = knit;

P = purl;

Psso = pass slipped stitch over;

Rem = remain(s)(ing);

Rep = repeat;

Rs = right side;

Sl 1 = slip one stitch;

St st (stockinette st) = stocking stitch (stockinette stitch) (k on rs rows, p on ws rows);

St(s) = stitch(es);

Tog = together;

Ws = wrong side;

Yfwd = yarn forward;

Yrn = yarn round needle.

Rosebud 5 sts = over next 5 sts, 3 long loops are pulled up to form rosebud effect.

Work these 5 sts as follows: K1, insert right needle point into centre of 3rd st of this group of 5 sts but 4 rows below and draw a loop through and leave this loop on right needle, K2, insert right needle point into centre of same st as used for last long loop and draw a 2nd loop through and leave this loop on right needle, K2, insert right needle point into centre of same st as used for last long loop and draw a 3rd loop through and leave this loop on right needle.

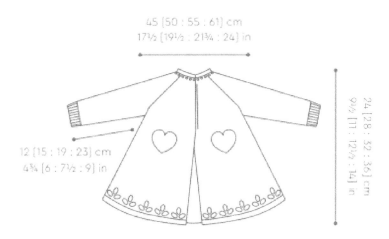

45 [50 : 55 : 61] cm
17½ [19½ : 21¾ : 24] in

12 [15 : 19 : 23] cm
4¾ [6 : 7½ : 9] in

24 [28 : 32 : 36] cm
9½ [11 : 12½ : 14] in

Instructions

BACK

Cast on 62 [70: 78: 86] sts using 3¾mm (UK 9 - US 5) needles.

Row 1 (rs) K2, *P2, K2, rep from * to end.

Row 2 P2, *K2, P2, rep from * to end. These 2 rows form rib. Work in rib for 2 rows more, dec [dec: inc: inc] 1 st at centre of last row and ending with a ws row. 61 [69: 79: 87] sts. Change to 4mm (UK 8 - US 6) needles. Beg with a K row, work in st st (stockinette st) for 6 rows, dec 1 st at each end of 3rd [5th: 3rd: 5th] of these rows and ending with a ws row. 59 [67: 77: 85] sts.

Next row (rs) K2 [6: 1: 5], (rosebud 5 sts, K5) 5 [5: 7: 7] times, rosebud 5 sts, K2 [6: 1: 5].

Next row P2 [6: 1: 5], *(P tog drawn up loop of previous row and next st, P1) twice, P tog drawn up loop of previous row and next st, P5, rep from * 4 [4: 6: 6] times more, (P tog drawn up loop of previous row and next st, P1) twice, P tog drawn up loop of previous row and next st, P2 [6: 1: 5]. Beg with a K row, cont in st st (stockinette st), dec 1 st at each end of next [3rd: next: 3rd] and 1 [2: 4: 5] foll 6th rows. 55 [61: 67: 73] sts. Work 3 rows, ending with a ws row.

Now place Heart Motifs as follows:

Next row (rs) K9 [11: 13: 15], work next 13 sts as row 1 of Heart Motif Chart, K11 [13: 15: 17], work next 13 sts as row 1 of Heart Motif Chart, K9 [11: 13: 15].

Next row P9 [11: 13: 15], work next 13 sts as row 2 of Heart Motif Chart, P11 [13: 15: 17], work next 13 sts as row 2 of Heart Motif Chart, P9 [11: 13: 15]. These 2 rows set the sts – 2 Heart Motifs with st st (stockinette st) between and at sides.

Keeping sts correct as now set, working rem 14 rows of Heart Motifs, cont as follows: Dec 1 st at each end of next and 2 foll 6th rows. 49 [55: 61: 67] sts. Work 1 row, ending after Heart Motif Chart row 16 and with a ws row.

Now working all sts in st st (stockinette st), beg with a K row, complete back as follows: Work 2 rows, ending with a ws row.

Shape raglan armholes

Cast (bind) off 3 sts at beg of next 2 rows. 43 [49: 55: 61] sts. Dec 1 st at each end of next and 3 [2: 2: 1] foll 4th rows, then on every foll alt row until 17 [19: 21: 23] sts rem. Work 1 row, ending with a ws row. Break yarn and leave sts on a holder (for Neckband).

LEFT FRONT

Cast on 32 [36: 40: 44] sts using 3¾mm (UK 9 - US 5) needles.

Row 1 (rs) *K2, P2, rep from * to last 4 sts, K4.

Row 2 *K2, P2, rep from * to end. These 2 rows set the sts – front opening edge 2 sts in g st with all other sts in rib.

Cont as set for 2 rows more, dec 1 [1: 0: 0] st at centre of last row and ending with a ws row. 31 [35: 40: 44] sts.

Change to 4mm (UK 8 - US 6) needles.

Row 5 (rs) knit. Row 6 K2, P to end. These 2 rows set the sts – front opening edge 2 sts still in g st with all other sts now in st st (stockinette st). Keeping sts correct as now set, work 4 rows, dec 1 st at beg of 1st [3rd: 1st: 3rd] of these rows and ending with a ws row. 30 [34: 39: 43] sts.

Next row (rs) K2 [6: 1: 5], (rosebud 5 sts, K5) 2 [2: 3: 3] times, rosebud 5 sts, K3.

Next row K2, P1, *(P tog drawn up loop of previous row and next st, P1) twice, P tog drawn up loop of previous row and next st, P5, rep from * 1 [1: 2: 2] times more, (P tog drawn up loop of previous row and next st, P1) twice, P tog drawn up loop of previous row and next st, P2 [6: 1: 5]. Now working all sts in st st (stockinette st) with front opening edge 2 sts in g st (as set by rows 5 and 6), cont as follows: Dec 1 st at beg of next [3rd: next: 3rd] and 1 [2: 4: 5] foll 6th rows. 28 [31: 34: 37] sts. Work 3 rows, ending with a ws row.

Now place Heart Motif as follows:

Next row (rs) K9 [11: 13: 15], work next 13 sts as row 1 of Heart Motif Chart, K6 [7: 8: 9].

Next row K2, P4 [5: 6: 7], work next 13 sts as row 2 of Heart Motif Chart, P9 [11: 13: 15]. These 2 rows set the sts – 1 heart motif with st st (stockinette st) at sides, and front opening edge 2 sts still in g st. Keeping sts correct as now set, working rem 14 rows of Heart Motifs, cont as follows: Dec 1 st at beg of next and 2 foll 6th rows. 25 [28: 31: 34] sts. Work 1 row, ending after Heart Motif Chart row 16 and with a ws row.

Now working all sts in st st (stockinette st) with front opening edge 2 sts still in g st, complete left front as follows:

Work 2 rows, ending with a ws row.

Shape raglan armhole

Cast (bind) off 3 sts at beg of next row. 22 [25: 28: 31] sts. Work 1 row. Dec 1 st at raglan armhole edge of next and 3 [2: 2: 1] foll 4th rows, then on every foll alt row until 15 [16: 18: 19] sts rem. Work 1 row, ending with a ws row.

Shape front neck

Next row (rs) k2tog, K to last 3 [4: 4: 5] sts and turn, leaving last 3 [4: 4: 5] sts on a holder (for Neckband). 11 [11: 13: 13] sts. Dec 1 st at raglan armhole edge of 2nd and foll 3 [3: 4: 4] alt rows and at same time dec 1 st at neck edge of next 4 rows, then on foll 1 [1: 2: 2] alt rows. 2 sts. Work 1 row, ending with a ws row.

Next row (rs) k2tog and fasten off

RIGHT FRONT

Cast on 32 [36: 40: 44] sts using 3¾mm (UK 9 - US 5) needles.

Row 1 (rs) K4, *P2, K2, rep from * to end. Row 2 *P2, K2, rep from * to end. These 2 rows set the sts – front opening edge 2 sts in g st with all other sts in rib.

Cont as set for 2 rows more, dec 1 [1: 0: 0] st at centre of last row and ending with a ws row. 31 [35: 40: 44] sts. Change to 4mm (UK 8 - US 6) needles.

Row 5 (rs) knit.

Row 6 P to last 2 sts, K2. These 2 rows set the sts – front opening edge 2 sts still in g st with all other sts now in st st (stockinette st). Keeping sts correct as now set, work 4 rows, dec 1 st at end of 1st [3rd: 1st: 3rd] of these rows and ending with a ws row. 30 [34: 39: 43] sts.

Next row (rs) K3, (rosebud 5 sts, K5) 2 [2: 3: 3] times, rosebud 5 sts, K2 [6: 1: 5].

Next row P2 [6: 1: 5], *(P tog drawn up loop of previous row and next st, P1) twice, P tog drawn up loop of previous row and next st, P5, rep from * 1 [1: 2: 2] times more, (P tog drawn up loop of previous row and next st, P1) twice, P tog drawn up loop of previous row and next st, P1, K2. Now working all sts in st st (stockinette st) with front opening edge 2 sts in g st (as set by rows 5 and 6), cont as follows: Dec 1 st at end of next [3rd: next: 3rd] and 1 [2: 4: 5] foll 6th rows. 28 [31: 34: 37] sts. Work 3 rows, ending with a ws row. Now place Heart Motif as follows:

Next row (rs) K6 [7: 8: 9], work next 13 sts as row 1 of Heart Motif Chart, K9 [11: 13: 15].

Next row P9 [11: 13: 15], work next 13 sts as row 2 of Heart Motif Chart, P4 [5: 6: 7], K2. These 2 rows set the sts – 1 heart motif with st st (stockinette st) at sides, and front opening edge 2 sts still in g st. Keeping sts correct as now set, working rem 14 rows of Heart Motifs, cont as follows:

Dec 1 st at end of next and 2 foll 6th rows. 25 [28: 31: 34] sts.

Work 1 row, ending after Heart Motif Chart row 16 and with a ws row.

Now working all sts in st st (stockinette st) with front opening edge 2 sts still in g st, complete right front as follows:

Work 2 rows, ending with a ws row.

Shape raglan armhole

Work 1 row.

Cast (bind) off 3 sts at beg of next row. 22 [25: 28: 31] sts.

Dec 1 st at raglan armhole edge of next and 3 [2: 2: 1] foll 4th rows, then on every foll alt row until 15 [16: 18: 19] sts rem.

Work 1 row, ending with a ws row.

Shape front neck

Next row (rs) K3 [4: 4: 5] and slip these sts onto a holder (for Neckband), K to last 2 sts, k2tog. 11 [11: 13: 13] sts.

Dec 1 st at raglan armhole edge of 2nd and foll 3 [3: 4: 4] alt rows and at same time dec 1 st at neck edge of next 4 rows, then on foll 1 [1: 2: 2] alt rows. 2 sts. Work 1 row, ending with a ws row.

Next row (rs) k2tog and fasten off.

SLEEVES

Cast on 25 [27: 29: 31] sts using 3¾mm (UK 9 - US 5) needles.

Row 1 (rs) K1, *P1, K1, rep from * to end.

Row 2 P1, *K1, P1, rep from * to end. These 2 rows form rib. Work in rib for 6 rows more, ending with a ws row. Change to 4mm (UK 8 - US 6) needles. Beg with a K row, work in st st (stockinette st) throughout as follows: Inc 1 st at each end of next and foll 8 [3: 0: 0] alt rows, then on 2 [7: 11: 5] foll 4th rows, then on 0 [0: 0: 6] foll 6th rows. 47 [49: 53: 55] sts. Work 3 [3: 5: 5] rows, ending with a ws row.

Shape raglan

Cast (bind) off 3 sts at beg of next 2 rows. 41 [43: 47: 49] sts. Dec 1 st at each end of next 3 rows, then on every foll alt row until 7 sts rem.

Work 1 row, ending with a ws row.

Break yarn and leave sts on a holder (for Neckband).

NECKBAND

Join all raglan seams.

With rs facing and using 3¼mm (UK 10 - US 3) needles, beg and ending at front opening edges, slip 3 [4: 4: 5] sts on right front holder onto right needle, rejoin yarn and pick up and knit 9 [9: 11: 11] sts up right side of front neck, K across 7 sts on right sleeve holder, then 17 [19: 21: 23] sts on back holder, and 7 sts on left sleeve holder, pick up and knit 9 [9: 11: 11] sts down left side of front neck, then K across 3 [4: 4: 5] sts on left front holder. 55 [59: 65: 69] sts.

Row 1 (ws) knit.

Row 2 knit.

Row 3 k1, p1, *yrn, p2tog, rep from * to last st, k1.

Row 4 knit. Cast (bind) off all sts knitwise (on ws).

MAKING UP

Do NOT steam press! Join side and sleeve seams.

Attach button to end of Neckband, using eyelet hole at opposite end of row 3 as buttonhole.

Pin out Matinee Jacket to measurements given, cover with a clean damp cloth and leave to dry naturally

Heart Motif

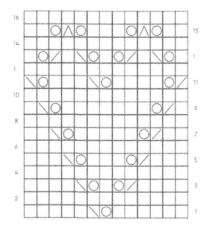

Key

K on rs rows,
P on ws rows

⊘ yfwd

⊘ K2tog

⊘ sl 1, K1, psso

⊘ sl 1, K2tog, psso

60

IV. Knit Sleepy Sack

MATERIALS

Bernat® Baby Blanket Tiny™ (3.5 oz/100 g; 316 yds/288 m)

Contrast A Snow Cap (14019) 2 balls

Bernat® Pipsqueak™ (3.5 oz/100 g; 101 yds/92 m) Contrast B

Baby Blue (59128) 2 balls

Sizes U.S. 6 (4 mm) and U.S. 9 (5.5 mm) knitting needles or size needed to obtain gauge.

Stitch holder.

2 buttons, 1½" [4 cm] in diameter.

5 yds (4.5 m) of black worsted weight yarn for embroidery.

ABBREVIATIONS

Alt = Alternate

Approx = Approximately

Beg = Begin(ing)

Cont = Continue

Dec = Decrease(ing)

K = Knit

K2tog = Knit next 2 stitches together

M1 = Make 1 stitch by picking up horizontal loop lying before next stitch and knitting into back of loop

P = Purl

P2tog = Purl next 2 stitches together

P2togtbl = Purl next 2 stitches together through back loops

Rem = Remain(ing)

Rep = Repeat

RS = Right side

Ssk = Slip next 2 stitches knitwise one at a time. Pass them back onto left-hand needle, then knit through back loops together.

St(s) = Stitch(es)

Tog = Together

WS = Wrong side

MEASUREMENTS

One size to fit baby 3-6 mos

Unfolded: Approx 25" [63.5 cm] square.

Folded: Approx 35" [89 cm] tall (from top of hood to bottom point) x 14" (35.5 cm] wide.

GAUGES

Bernat® Blanket Tiny™ 18 sts and 24 rows = 4" [10 cm] in stocking st with smaller needles.

Bernat® Pipsqueak™ 11 sts and 16 rows = 4" [10 cm] in stocking stitch with larger needles.

INSTRUCTIONS

BACK

**With smaller needles and A, cast on 26 sts.

1st row: (RS). K1. M1.

Knit to last st. M1. K1. 28 sts.

2nd and alt rows: Purl.

Rep last 2 rows 15 times more. 58 sts.

Beg on a knit row, work even in stocking st until piece from beg measures 26" [66 cm], ending on a purl row.

Shape armholes:

Cast off 4 sts beg next 2 rows. 50 sts.

** Work even in stocking st until armhole measures 5" [12.5 cm], ending on a purl row.

Straps

1st row: K15. Slip last 15 sts just worked onto a st holder.

Cast off next 20 sts loosely. K15.

Turn.

***Beg on a purl row, work even in stocking st on these 15 sts until Strap measures 4½" [11.5 cm], ending on a purl row.

Buttonhole row:

1st row: (RS). K6. Cast off 3 sts. K6.

2nd row: Purl, casting on 3 sts overcast off sts. 15 sts.

Next row: ssk. Knit to last 2 sts. K2tog. 13 sts.

Next row: P2tog. Purl to last 2 sts. P2togtbl. 11 sts.

Rep last 2 rows once more. 7 sts.

Cast off knitwise.***

With WS facing, slip rem 15 sts onto needle.

With A, work from *** to *** as given for first Strap.

FRONT

Work from ** to ** as given for Back.

Beg on a knit row, work even in stocking st until armhole measures 3½" [9 cm], ending on a purl row.

Right Front:

Shape neck:

1st row: (RS). K20. K2tog (neck edge).

Turn.

Leave rem sts on spare needle.

2nd row: P2tog. Purl to end of row. 20 sts.

3rd row: K18. K2tog. Turn. 19 sts.

4th row: Purl.

Cont dec 1 st at neck edge on RS rows only to 15 sts.

Next row: Purl.

Cast off knitwise.

Left Front:

1st row: With RS facing, A and smaller needles, cast off next 6 sts.

ssk. Knit to end of row. 21 sts.

2nd row: P19. P2togtbl. 20 sts.

3rd row: ssk. Knit to end of row. 19 sts.

4th row: Purl.

Cont dec 1 st at neck edge on RS rows only to 15 sts.

Next row: Purl.

Cast off knitwise.

LINING BACK

**With larger needles and B, cast on 14 sts.

1st row: (RS). K1. M1. Knit to last st. M1. K1. 16 sts.

2nd and alt rows: Purl.

Rep last 2 rows 9 times more. 34 sts.

Beg on a knit row, work even in stocking st until work from beg measures 26" [66 cm], ending on a purl row.

Shape armholes:

Cast off 3 sts beg next 2 rows. 28 sts.

** Work even in stocking st until armhole measures 5" [12.5 cm], ending on a purl row.

Straps

1st row: K8. Slip last 8 sts just worked onto a st holder.

Cast off next 12 sts loosely. K8.

Turn.

***Beg on a purl row, work even in stocking st on these 8 sts until Strap measures 4½" [11.5 cm], ending on a purl row.

Buttonhole row:

1st row: (RS). K3. Cast off 2 sts. K3.

2nd row: Purl, casting on 2 sts over cast off sts. 8 sts.

3rd row: ssk. Knit to last 2 sts. K2tog. 6 sts.

4th row: P2tog. Purl to last 2 sts. P2togtbl. 4 sts.

Cast off knitwise.

***With WS facing, slip rem 8 sts onto needle. Join B and work from *** to *** as given for first Strap.

LINING FRONT

Work from ** to ** as given for Lining Back.

Work even in stocking st until armhole measures 3½" [9 cm], ending on a purl row.

Right Front:

Shape neck:

1st row: (RS). K10. K2tog (neck edge).

Turn.

Leave rem sts on spare needle.

2nd row: P2tog. Purl to end of row. 10 sts.

3rd row: K8. K2tog. 9 sts.

4th row: Purl.

5th row: K7. K2tog. 8 sts.

6th row: Purl. Cast off knitwise.

Left Front:

1st row: With RS facing, B and larger needles, cast off next 4 sts. ssk. Knit to end of row. 11 sts.

2nd row: P9. P2togtbl. 10 sts.

3rd row: ssk. Knit to end of row. 9 sts.

4th row: Purl.

5th row: K7. K2tog. 8 sts.

6th row: Purl.

Cast off knitwise.

FINISHING

With black worsted weight yarn, embroider eyes and eyelashes using chain stitch as shown in photo.

Using mattress st, sew Lining to Front and Back along top to beg of armhole shaping.

Sew Lining only along side and bottom seams.

Sew side and bottom seams of Back and Front, tacking Lining into place on the inside along bottom.

Sew buttons to Front straps to correspond to buttonholes.

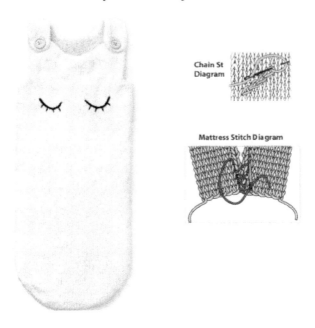

Chain St Diagram

Mattress Stitch Diagram

V. Very Scary Knit Pullovers

MATERIALS

Bernat® Super Value™ (7 oz/197 g; 440 yds/402 m) Sizes 2 4 6 8 years

Skull Version

Main Color (MC) Black (07421) 1 2 2 2 ball(s) Contrast A

White (07391) 1 1 1 1 ball

Jack-O'-Lantern Version

Main Color (MC) Carrot (00615) 1 2 2 2 ball(s) Contrast A

Yellow (07445) 1 1 1 1 ball

Sizes U.S. 7 (4.5 mm) and U.S. 8 (5 mm) knitting needles or size

needed to obtain gauge.

2 st holders.

ABBREVIATIONS

Alt = Alternate

Beg = Begin(ning)

Cont = Continue(ity)

Dec = Decrease(ing)

Inc = Increase(ing)

K = Knit

Pat = Pattern

Rem = Remain(ing)

Rep = Repeat

RS = Right side

St(s) = Stitch(es)

Tog = Together

WS = Wrong side

SIZES

To fit chest measurement

2 21" [53.5 cm]

4 23" [58.5 cm]

6 25" [63.5 cm]

8 26½" [67.5 cm]

Length from shoulder to hem

2 25" [63.5 cm]

4 27" [68.5 cm]

6 29½" [75 cm]

8 32½" [82.5 cm]

GAUGE

18 sts and 24 rows = 4" [10 cm] with larger needles in stocking st.

INSTRUCTIONS

The instructions are written for smallest size.

If changes are necessary for larger sizes the instructions will be written thus ().

When only one number is given, it applies to all sizes.

For ease in working, circle all numbers pertaining to your size.

BACK

**With MC and smaller needles, cast on 57 (61-67-73)sts.

1st row: (RS). K1. *P1. K1. Rep from * to end of row.

2nd row: P1. *K1. P1. Rep from * to end of row. Rep last 2 rows of (K1. P1) ribbing for 2" [5 cm], ending on a 2nd row.**

Change to larger needles and proceed in stocking st until work from beg measures 7½ (8-9-11)" [19 (20.5-23-28) cm], ending with a purl row.

Shape armholes:

Cast off 4 (4- 6-6) sts beg next 2 rows. 49 (53- 55-61) sts. Cont even until armhole measures 5½ (6-6½-7)" [14 (15-16.5-18) cm], ending with a purl row.

Shape shoulders:

Cast off 6 (6- 6-8) sts beg next 2 rows, then cast off 6 (7-7-8) sts beg following 2 rows.

Leave rem 25 (27-29-29) sts on a st holder.

FRONT

Note: When working from chart, wind small balls of the colors to be used, one for each separate area of color in the design.

Start new colors at appropriate points. To change colors, twist the two yarns around each other where they meet on WS to avoid a hole.

Work from ** to ** as given for Back.

Jack-o'-Lantern Version only:

Change to larger needles and proceed in stocking st for 4 (6- 10-14) rows.

Place chart:

1st row: (RS). K9 (11- 14-17). Work 1st row of Chart I across next 39 sts. Knit to end of row.

2nd row: P 9 (11-14-17). Work 2nd row of Chart I across next 39 sts. Purl to end of row. See Chart I

Skull and Crossbones Version only: Change to larger needles and proceed in stocking st for 2 (4- 8-12) rows.

Place chart:

1st row: (RS). K10 (12-15-18). Work 1st row of Chart II across next 37 sts. Knit to end of row.

2nd row: P10 (12-15-18). Work 2nd row of Chart II across next 37 sts. Purl to end of row. See Chart II.

Both Versions: Keeping cont of chart, as placed in last 2 rows, cont even until work from beg measures same length as Back to armholes, ending with a purl row.

Shape armholes: Cast off 4 (4- 6-6) sts beg next 2 rows. 49 (53- 55-61) sts. Cont even until armhole measures 3½ (3½-4-4½)" [9 (9-10-11.5) cm], ending with a purl row.

Shape neck:

Next row: K18 (20- 20-23) (neck edge). Turn. Leave rem sts on a spare needle. Dec 1 st at neck edge on next 4 rows, then on every following alt row 2 (3-3-3) times. 12 (13-13-16) sts. Cont even until armhole measures same length as Back to beg of shoulder shaping, ending with a purl row.

Shape shoulder: Cast off 6 (6- 6-8) sts beg next row. Work 1 row even. Cast off rem 7 (7-7-8) sts. With RS of work facing, slip next 13 (13-15-15) sts onto a st holder. Join MC to rem sts and knit to end of row. Dec 1 st at neck edge on next 4 rows, then on every following alt row 2 (3-3-3) times. 12 (13-13-16) sts. Cont even until armhole measures same length as Back to beg of shoulder shaping, ending with a purl row.

Shape shoulder:

Cast off 6 (6- 6-8) sts beg next row.

Work 1 row even.

Cast off rem 7 (7-7-8) sts.

SLEEVES

With MC and smaller needles, cast on 33 (35-35-37) sts.

Work 2" [5 cm] in (K1. P1) ribbing as given for Back, inc 4 sts evenly across last row. 37 (39-39-41) sts.

Change to larger needles and proceed in stocking st for 4 rows. Inc 1 st each end of needle on next and every following 4th row until there are 41 (47-47-53) sts, then on every following 6th row until there are 49 (55-59-63) sts.

Cont even until work from beg measures 8½ (10-11½-13)" [21.5 (25.5-29-33) cm], ending with a purl row. Place markers at each end of last row.

Work 4 (4-6-6) rows even.

Cast off.

FINISHING

Pin garment pieces to measurements. Cover with a damp cloth, leaving cloth to dry.

Neckband: Sew right shoulder seam. With RS of work facing and smaller needles, pick up and knit 13 (15-15-15) sts down left front neck edge. K13 (13-15-15) from front st holder. Pick up and knit 13 (15-15-15) sts up right front neck edge. K25 (27-29-29) from back st holder, inc 1 st at center. 65 (71-75-75) sts. Beg on a 2nd row, work 7 rows in (K1. P1) ribbing as given for Back.

Cast off in ribbing.

Sew left shoulder and neckband. Sew in sleeves placing rows above markers along cast off sts of front and back to form square armholes. Sew side and sleeve seams

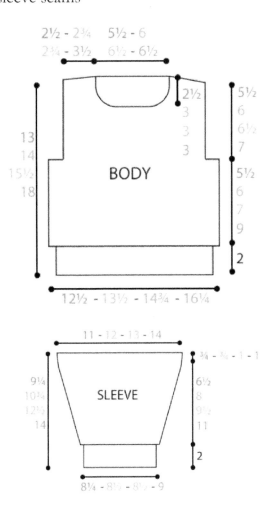

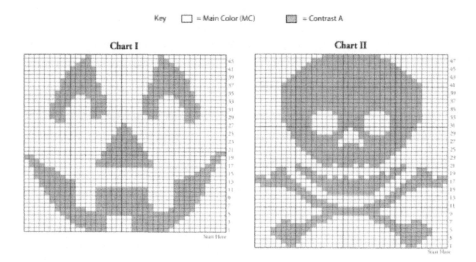

Key   ☐ = Main Color (MC)   ▦ = Contrast A

Chart I   **Chart II**

VI. Little Man Cable Cardigan

MATERIALS

RED HEART® Baby Hugs™

Medium: 3 (3, 3, 3, 5) balls 4315

Teddy Susan Bates®

Knitting Needles: 5.5 mm [US 9] 4 (5, 5, 5) buttons 1" (2.5 cm) diameter, cable needle, 2 stitch holders, yarn needle

GAUGE:

14 sts = 4" (10 cm); 27 rows = 4" (10 cm) in Garter Ridge pattern. 20 sts = 4" (10 cm); 21 rows = 4" (10 cm) in Cable pattern.

CHECK YOUR GAUGE. Use any size needles to obtain the gauge

Directions are for size 2 years.

Changes for sizes 4 years, 6 years, and 8 years are in parentheses.

Finished Chest:

24½ (26½, 28½, 30½)" (62 (67.5, 72.5, 77.5) cm, buttoned

Finished Length:

14½ (16, 18, 20)" (37 (40.5, 45.5, 51) cm

Notes

1. Body of cardigan is worked in one piece beginning at lower edge. Piece is divided at underarms and back and fronts worked separately to shoulders. Front bands are also worked separately to center back neck.

2. Sleeves are worked separately and sewn into armholes.

ABBREVIATIONS

k = knit

k2tog = knit next 2 sts together

p = purl

p2tog = purl next 2 sts together

st(s) = stitch(es)

yo = yarn over

[ ] = work directions in brackets the number of times specified

* = repeat whatever follows the * as indicated.

Special Stitches

seed-back 3/3 RC (3 over 3 seed sts right cross) = Slip next 3 stitches to cable needle and hold in back, k3, then k1, p1, k1 from cable needle.

seed-front 3/3 RC (3 seed sts over 3 right cross) = Slip next 3 stitches to cable needle and hold in back, k1, p1, k1, then k3 from cable needle.

M1 = Make 1 (Increase) – Lift strand between needles to left-hand needle and work strand through the back loop, twisting it to prevent a hole, [knit or purl as indicated by pattern st].

Pattern Stitches Buttonhole (over 9 sts)

Row 1: Work in Garter Ridge pattern as established over next 3 sts, work next 2 sts tog (k2tog or p2tog to match pattern), yo, work in

Garter Ridge pattern as established over next 4 sts..

Cable Pattern (over 10 sts)

Row 1 (wrong side): *P1, k1, p3, k1, p1, k2, p1; repeat from * across.

Row 2: *[K1, p1] twice, k4, p1, k1; repeat from * across.

Rows 3–6: Repeat Rows 1 and 2 twice.

Row 7: Repeat Row 1.

Row 8: *K1, p1, seed-back 3/3 RC, p1, k1; repeat from * across.

Row 9: *P1, k2, p1, k1, p3, k1, p1; repeat from * across.

Row 10: *K1, p1, k4, [p1, k1] twice; repeat from * across.

Rows 11–14: Repeat Rows 9 and 10 twice.

Row 15: Repeat Row 9.

Row 16: *K1, p1, seed-front 3/3 RC, p1, k1; repeat from * across.

Repeat Rows 1–16 for Cable pattern.

Garter Ridge Pattern

Row 1 (wrong side): Knit.

Row 2: Knit.

Rows 3 and 4: Purl. Repeat Rows 1–4 for Garter Ridge pattern.

BODY

Cast on 128 (138, 148, 158) sts.

Row 1 (wrong side): Work Row 1 of Garter Ridge pattern over first 9 sts, place marker, work Row 1 of Cable pattern to last 9 sts, place marker, work Row 1 of Garter Ridge pattern to end of row.

Rows 2–4: Work in Garter Ridge pattern to first marker, slip marker, work in Cable pattern to next marker, slip marker, work in Garter Ridge pattern to end of row.

Row 5 (buttonhole row): If making girl's cardigan work in Garter Ridge pattern to first marker, if making boy's cardigan work Buttonhole over first 9 sts, slip marker, work in Cable pattern to next marker, slip marker, if making boy's cardigan work in Garter Ridge pattern to end of row, if making girl's cardigan work Buttonhole over last 9 sts. Work even in pattern as established for 13 (11, 13, 15) rows. Repeat Row 5 (buttonhole row). Repeat last 14 (12, 14, 16) rows 1 (2, 2, 2) more times (for a total of 3 (4, 4, 4) buttonholes). Work even in pattern as established for 13 (11, 13, 15) rows.

Left Front

Notes:

1. When instructed to "decrease 1 st" work k2tog or p2tog, whichever you prefer, to match the current pattern.

2. The fronts are longer than the back. The shoulder seam will lie at the back of the shoulder, slightly below the natural shoulder line.

Row 1 (wrong side): If making girl's cardigan work in Garter Ridge pattern to first marker, if making boy's cardigan work Buttonhole over first 9 sts, remove marker and place these 9 sts on a holder (for left front band), work in Cable pattern over next 22 (24, 26, 29) sts, decrease 1 st; place remaining sts on another holder for back and right front—23 (25, 27, 30) sts.

Row 2: Decrease 1 st (armhole edge decrease), work in Cable pattern as established to last 2 sts, decrease 1 st (neck edge decrease)—21 (23, 25, 28) sts.

Row 3: Work in Cable pattern as established to last 2 sts, decrease 1 st (armhole edge decrease)—20 (22, 24, 27) sts.

Row 4: Work in Cable pattern as established to last 2 sts, decrease 1 st (neck edge decrease)—19 (21, 23, 26) sts.

Row 5: Work even in Cable pattern as established.

Rows 6–11 (13, 15, 17): Repeat last 2 rows 3 (4, 5, 6) more times—16 (17, 18, 20) sts remain. Work even in patterns as established until armhole measures about 6 (6½, 7, 7½)" (15 (16.5, 18, 19) cm).

Bind off.

Back

Row 1 (WS): With wrong side facing, join yarn at beginning of stitches on holder, decrease 1 st, work in Cable pattern as established over next 58 (64, 70, 74) sts, decrease 1 st; leave remaining sts on holder for right front—60 (66, 72, 76) sts.

Rows 2 and 3 (decrease rows): Decrease 1 st, work in Cable pattern as established to last 2 sts, decrease 1 st—56 (62, 68, 72) sts. Work even in Cable pattern as established for 24 (26, 28, 30) more rows. Bind off.

Right Front

Row 1 (WS): With wrong side facing, join yarn at beginning of stitches on holder, decrease 1 st, work in Cable pattern as established to marker, slip marker, if making boy's cardigan work in Garter Ridge pattern to end of row, if making girl's cardigan work Buttonhole over last 9 sts.

Row 2: Work in Garter Ridge pattern to marker, remove marker and place these 9 sts on a holder (for right front band), decrease 1 st (neck edge decrease), work in Cable pattern as established to last 2 sts, decrease 1 st (armhole edge decrease)—21 (23, 25, 28) sts.

Row 3: Decrease 1 st (armhole edge decrease), work in Cable pattern as established to end of row—20 (22, 24, 27) sts.

Row 4: Decrease 1 st (neck edge decrease), work in Cable pattern as established to end of row—19 (21, 23, 26) sts.

Row 5: Work even in patterns as established.

Rows 6–11 (13, 15, 17): Repeat last 2 rows 3 (4, 5, 6) more times—16 (17, 18, 20) sts remain.

Work even in patterns as established until right front measures same as left front.

Bind off. If desired, block piece by misting and let dry.

Do not use heat, because the cables and ridges will flatten. Sew shoulder seams.

Left Front Band

Return left front band sts from holder to needle, ready to work a right side row. Work even in Garter Ridge pattern as established for 4 rows. Increase Row (right side): Work first st, M1, continue in Garter Ridge pattern to end of row—10 sts. Work even in Garter Ridge pattern for 3 rows. Repeat Increase Row—11 sts. Repeat last 4 rows 3 more times—14 sts. Work even in Garter Ridge pattern until band comfortably reaches slightly past center back neck; end with a Row 1 or Row 3 of pattern. Place sts on a holder. Cut yarn.

Right Front Band

Return right front band sts from holder to needle, ready to work a wrong side row.

Work even in Garter Ridge pattern as established for 3 rows.

Increase Row (right side): Work in Garter Ridge pattern to last st, M1, work last st—10 sts. Repeat last 4 rows 4 more times—14 sts. Work even in Garter Ridge pattern until band comfortably reaches slightly past center back neck; end with same row of pattern as left front band. Graft ends of front bands together. Sew long inner edge of front bands to neck edge of cardigan, easing in fullness of band at back of neck.

SLEEVES (make 2)

Cast on 28 (30, 32, 34) sts.

Size 2 years Only:

Row 1 (wrong side): P1, k2, p1, work in Cable pattern to last 4 sts, p1, k1, p2.

Row 2: K2, p1, k1, work in Cable pattern to last 4 sts, [k1, p1] twice.

Size 4 years Only:

Row 1 (wrong side): Work in Cable pattern to end of row.

Row 2: Work in Cable pattern to end of row.

Size 6 years Only:

Row 1 (wrong side): P1, work in Cable pattern to last st, p1.

Row 2: K1, work in Cable pattern to last st, k1.

Size 8 years Only:

Row 1 (wrong side): K1, p1, work in Cable pattern to last 2 sts, p1, k1.

Row 2: P1, k1, work in Cable pattern to last 2 sts, k1, p1.

All Sizes:

Notes:

You will now continue in pattern as established. As stitches are increased, incorporate the new stitches into the Cable pattern.

Do not work any crosses in the new stitches until a sufficient number of stitches have been increased.

Work even in Cable pattern as established for 1 (1, 3, 3) rows.

Increase Row (right side):

Work in Cable pattern as established and increase 1 st at beginning and end of row—30 (32, 34, 36) sts. Work even in Cable pattern as established for 3 (3, 5, 5) rows. Repeat Increase Row—32 (34, 36, 38) sts. Repeat last 4 (4, 6, 6) rows 7 (7, 7, 8) more times—46 (48, 50, 54) sts. Work even in Cable pattern as established until piece measures about 8½ (10½, 11½, 12½)" (21.5 (26.5, 29, 32) cm) from beginning.

Shape Cap

Next 12 (14, 16, 20) Rows: Work in Cable pattern as established and decrease 1 st at beginning and end of each row—22 (20, 18, 14) sts. Bind off.

FINISHING

If desired, block sleeves but only lightly.

Sew sleeve seams and sew sleeves into armholes.

Sew buttons opposite buttonholes.

Weave in any remaining ends.

VII. Princess Blanket

MATERIALS

Red Heart® Soft Baby Steps®: 4 balls 9800

Baby Blue OR 9700 Baby Pink. Susan Bates® Circular

Knitting Needles: 5mm [US 8] – 36" (91.4 cm)

Yarn needle

Gauge: 14 sts = 3" (7.6 cm); 21 rows = 4" (10 cm) in pattern.

CHECK YOUR GAUGE. Use any size needle to obtain the gauge

Blanket measures 35" x 31" (89 x 78.5 cm)

ABBREVIATIONS

K = knit

K2tog = knit two together

mm = millimeters

P = purl

P2tog = purl two together

st(s) = stitch(es)

yo = yarn over

* or ** = repeat whatever follows the * or ** as indicated

[ ] = work directions in brackets the number of times specified

Special Abbreviation

Loop = [Move st on right needle back to left needle, K1] two times.

INSTRUCTIONS

BLANKET

Cast on 121 sts.

Row 1 (Right Side): K8; [P7, K7] eight times; K1.

Row 2: P8; [K7, P7] eight times; P1.

Row 3: K4, yo, K2tog, K2; [P3, yo, P2tog, P2, K3, yo, K2tog, K2] eight times; K1.

Row 4: Repeat Row 2.

Row 5: K2, K2tog, yo, K1, yo, K2tog, K1; [P1, P2tog, yo, P1, yo, P2tog, P1, K1, K2tog, yo, K1, yo, K2tog, K1] eight times; K1.

Row 6: Repeat Row 2.

Row 7: K3, K2tog, yo, K3; [P2, P2tog, yo, P3, K2, K2tog, yo, K3] eight times; K1.

Row 8: Repeat Row 2.

Repeat Rows 2- 8 eighteen more times. Last Row: K8; [P7, K7] eight times; K1. Bind off all sts.

Shell Edging

Row 1 (Right Side): Beginning at bound-off edge, *[pick up and K6 sts across next square] 19 times; continuing along next side [pick up and K6 sts across next square] 16 times; pick up and K5 sts across next square; repeat from * one more time – 430 sts; place marker for beginning of row.

Row 2: Purl.

Row 3: K1; *work 5 sts in next st; turn; P5, slip next st, turn; K2tog; [Loop; K1, pass first stitch on needle over next st] three times;

Loop; K2tog, pass first stitch on needle over next st; bind off 3 sts; repeat from * to end. Fasten off. Weave in ends.

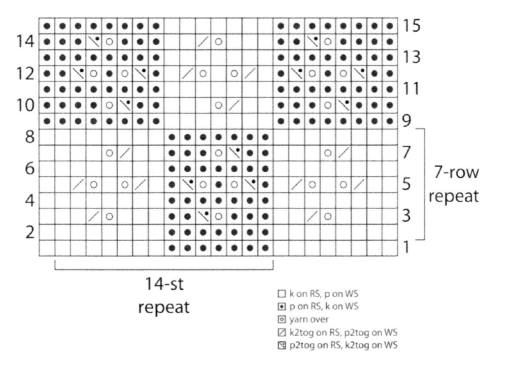

14-st
repeat

7-row
repeat

☐ k on RS, p on WS
☑ p on RS, k on WS
☑ yarn over
☑ k2tog on RS, p2tog on WS
☑ p2tog on RS, k2tog on WS

Printed in Great Britain
by Amazon

32206652R00056